Charles

Prince of Wales

Charles
Prince of Wales

GILL KNAPPETT

Inside cover: Queen Elizabeth II with her heir apparent, Prince Charles, and his heir, Prince William, photographed at Clarence House in 2003 before a dinner to mark the 50th anniversary of Her Majesty's coronation.
Title page: Two-year-old Prince Charles with his mother, Princess Elizabeth, at Clarence House.
Previous page left: The Prince of Wales making a speech at the Royal Albert Hall in 1983.
Previous page right: The Prince of Wales in 2016.

Publication in this form copyright © Pitkin Publishing 2018
Text © Pitkin Publishing 2018

Written by Gill Knappett (www.knappett.co.uk)
The moral right of the author has been asserted

Edited by Claire Handy
Picture research by Sarah Kay-Walker
Designed by Tatiana Losinska

All photographs by kind permission of PA Images

Select bibliography:
Prince Charles by Sally Bedell Smith; *Charles, The Heart of a King* by Catherine Mayer;
Charles, The Man Who Will Be King by Howard Hodgson. Pitkin guidebooks and the website
www.princeofwales.gov.uk have also been used for research purposes in the preparation of
this souvenir guide.

A CIP catalogue for this book is available from the British Library

Pitkin Publishing
43 Great Ormond Street, London WC1N 3HZ, UK
Sales and enquiries: +44 (0)20 7462 1506
Email: sales@pavilionbooks.com

An imprint of Pavilion Books Company Limited

Printed in Turkey
ISBN: 978-1-84165-784-4   1/18

CONTENTS

PRINCE CHARLES' TIMELINE

1948 Prince Charles Philip Arthur George is born on 14 November, the first child of Princess Elizabeth and Prince Philip, and second in line to the throne.

1952 King George VI dies in February and Prince Charles' mother accedes the throne as Queen Elizabeth II.

1956 After being taught at home, Prince Charles starts at Hill House School, Knightsbridge, but becomes a boarder at Cheam School in Hampshire the following year.

1958 The nine-year-old Charles learns that he is to become Prince of Wales.

1962 In May, Prince Charles starts his secondary education at Gordonstoun in Scotland.

1967 Prince Charles goes to Trinity College, Cambridge, graduating three years later.

1968 Prince Charles is invested as a Knight of the Garter at St George's Chapel, Windsor.

1969 Prince Charles is invested as the Prince of Wales at Caernarfon Castle on 1 July.

1971 The Prince of Wales begins his career in the services at RAF Cranwell, Lincolnshire in March; in September he starts at the Royal Naval College, Dartmouth.

1972 Prince Charles is introduced to Camilla Shand (later Mrs Parker Bowles) by a mutual friend.

1976 Prince Charles launches The Prince's Trust in June; after completing his final tour of duty, he leaves the Royal Navy in December.

1977 Prince Charles is introduced to 16-year-old Lady Diana Spencer by her sister.

1979 Prince Charles is devastated when his great-uncle, Earl Mountbatten of Burma, is killed; that same year Prince Charles founds the Prince of Wales' Charitable Foundation.

1980 The Highgrove Estate near Tetbury in Gloucestershire is purchased for Prince Charles by the Duchy of Cornwall.

1981 The Prince of Wales and Lady Diana Spencer are engaged in February and marry at St Paul's Cathedral on 29 July.

1982 Prince William Arthur Philip Louis, the first child of the Prince and Princess of Wales, and heir apparent, is born on 21 June.

1984 In May, Prince Charles famously speaks out about his concerns regarding the effect of modern British architecture on ordinary people; Prince Henry Charles Albert David (Harry) is born on 15 September, a brother to Prince William.

1993 Poundbury, an urban extension of Dorchester in Dorset, is started on land owned by the Duchy of Cornwall, and based on the architectural principle of Prince Charles.

1996 The Prince and Princess of Wales are divorced; Diana is killed in a car crash the following year.

2002 The Queen Mother dies aged 101; Prince Charles gives a moving tribute to his grandmother from Highgrove.

2005 Prince Charles and Camilla Parker Bowles are engaged in February and marry at Windsor in April; she is known by the title Duchess of Cornwall.

2013 Prince Charles becomes a grandfather for the first time when Prince George Alexander Louis is born on 22 July, the first child of the Duke and Duchess of Cambridge and third in line to the throne.

2014 It is announced that The Queen is to relinquish some of her royal duties, which are to be shared between her four children and Princes William and Harry.

2015 Prince Charles becomes a grandfather again when Princess Charlotte Elizabeth Diana is born on 2 May, a sister to Prince George.

Right: Polo-playing Prince Charles with his sons in 2001.

GOD BLESS THE PRINCE OF WALES

On 14 November 2018, HRH The Prince of Wales celebrates his 70th birthday. His is a long-awaited kingship, his status determined from birth.

He may have had a life of hierarchy, protocol and privilege, with values of discipline and order instilled since childhood by his family, the royal court and his schools, but it has not been a life spent waiting for his eventual role as King.

Less reticent by nature than his mother, Queen Elizabeth II, the Prince of Wales is known for his unwillingness to follow convention. He expresses his opinions and uses his influence to make the world a better place, determined to be known for his work rather than his birthright. As his wife, the Duchess of Cornwall, reports, he is a man who is rarely idle and 'not one for chilling'.

Along with his steadfast support for his mother and his exemplary talents as a goodwill ambassador for Britain, both nationally and internationally, this royal Prince is also known for his engaging smile, infectious chuckle, sense of humour and self-deprecating manner – qualities that help put people he meets at ease very quickly, and all welcome characteristics for a future monarch.

Whilst the words to this patriotic song may have been penned for the future King Edward VII in 1863, their message holds just as true for our own 21st-century heir to the throne:

Among our ancient mountains,
And from our lovely vales,
Oh! Let the prayer re-echo
God bless the Prince of Wales!

Left: The Prince of Wales meets well-wishers at the Sandringham Flower Show in July 2017.

A FUTURE KING IS BORN

'The Princess Elizabeth, Duchess of Edinburgh was safely delivered of a Prince at nine fourteen pm today. Her Royal Highness and her son are both doing well.'

The hand-written note attached to the Buckingham Palace railings by King George VI's press secretary on 14 November 1948 raised a cheer and a rendition of 'For He's a Jolly Good Fellow' from the crowds who had gathered outside as they waited for news of the royal birth.

That the 7lb 6oz baby was a boy meant that Princess Elizabeth and Prince Philip's firstborn would one day be monarch. Had the baby been a girl, she would have taken her place behind any future brothers in the line of succession, as dictated by the Succession to the Crown Act first formed in 1701 – an Act that was changed in 2013 to give girls born after 28 October 2011 equal succession rights.

Right: Princess Elizabeth with baby Prince Charles.

Unlike her son, Princess Elizabeth had not been born to reign. It was only the abdication of her uncle, Edward VIII, in December 1936, followed by the crowning of his younger brother, the Princess' father, as King George VI in 1937 that meant Elizabeth became first in line to the throne.

Left: Princess Elizabeth holds Prince Charles after his christening, flanked by the baby's great-grandmothers the Dowager Marchioness of Milford Haven (left) and Queen Mary (right). Standing left to right are his sponsors: Lady Brabourne; The Duke of Edinburgh (here representing Prince George of Greece as sponsor); King George VI; David Bowes-Lyon; the Earl of Athlone (representing King Haakon of Norway); and Princess Margaret.

The wedding of Princess Elizabeth and Prince Philip – newly titled the Duke of Edinburgh on his marriage – on 20 November 1947 had been just the tonic post-war Britain needed, and the arrival of their first child a year later only added to the nation's joy. Their son was the first royal baby to be born without the Home Secretary in attendance, as had been the tradition until that point. However, the boy was born at home – in the ornate Buhl Room at Buckingham Palace, converted into a delivery suite – rather than in hospital, a royal tradition that did not change until 1982.

Despite regular bulletins about the new arrival, one thing remained a mystery: his name. Speculation was rife, but the name of the next heir to the throne was not announced until his christening a full month later. On 15 December 1948, it finally became public knowledge: the baby was called Charles Philip Arthur George. Many people were surprised at the choice of the name Charles, which had not been used by the Royal Family for more than 300 years after the unhappy reigns of Charles I and Charles II.

The christening took place in the Music Room of Buckingham Palace, an imposing columned chamber with a high-domed ceiling and arched windows. The service was conducted by the Archbishop of Canterbury who baptised the Prince with water from the river Jordan in the silver-gilt Lily Font, commissioned by Queen Victoria and first used in 1841 for the christening of her first child.

HRH Prince Charles of Edinburgh, dressed in the Honiton lace christening gown worn by royal babies since the days of Queen Victoria, was surrounded by his parents, his maternal grandparents King George VI and Queen Elizabeth, maternal great-grandmother Queen Mary, paternal great-grandmother the Dowager Marchioness of Milford Haven, and his godparents, known as sponsors in royal circles.

A ROYAL UPBRINGING

In 1949 the three-strong family moved into the newly refurbished Clarence House, Charles safely established in his blue and white nursery and sleeping in a cot that had belonged to both his mother and his aunt, Princess Margaret.

Though his parents delighted in their baby son, the nursery was overseen by nanny Helen Lightbody, an experienced Scottish nanny with a strict manner, and her young assistant, Mabel Anderson. Mabel was 22 – the same age as Princess Elizabeth – when she replied to an advertisement for an assistant nanny, little knowing it was for the royal household. It was she who put the young Prince to bed, made sure he brushed his teeth, read him stories, taught him to say his prayers – and she he turned to if he fell and grazed a knee. Mabel (nicknamed 'Mipsy' by her young charge) was, in Prince Charles' words, 'a haven of security' and remained an important part of his life in adulthood.

The busy Princess Elizabeth was occasionally absent for extended periods during Charles' infancy. She spent time in Malta with Prince Philip when he was posted there in the autumn of 1949 as second-in-command of *Chequers*, the ship that led the first destroyer flotilla of the Mediterranean Fleet. The Princess celebrated her son's first birthday with him before flying to Malta to be with her husband for their second wedding anniversary. Young Charles remained at home in the care of his nannies and fond grandparents.

Right: A delighted Princess Elizabeth and the Duke of Edinburgh with six-month-old Prince Charles.

Far right: King George VI was recovering from a lung operation when he was photographed with Prince Charles at Buckingham Palace on his grandson's third birthday. One of the Prince's greatest regrets is never having a chance to really know his maternal grandfather, who died three months after this photograph was taken.

Left: Princess Elizabeth with Prince Charles and Princess Anne on the baby's first birthday, 15 August 1951.

On 15 August 1950, Prince Charles' sister was born at Clarence House. Charles, not yet two, was joined in the nursery by the baby, christened Anne Elizabeth Alice Louise. Their mother returned to Malta in November that year, soon after Charles' second birthday, where Prince Philip had been made lieutenant commander of the frigate *Magpie*.

Philip knew that his naval career was drawing to a close; his father-in-law's health was failing and plans were in place for the Edinburghs to make an official tour of Canada in autumn 1951. In July 1951, the young couple left Malta for the last time, Philip duty-bound to support his wife who was beginning to take on many of her parents' public engagements and whose workload was now considerable.

As Princess Anne grew, she and her elder brother became the best of playmates, despite their different natures. He was a thoughtful, shy and sensitive child; she a high-spirited tomboy. Their father gravitated naturally towards his boisterous, outgoing daughter whilst trying to encourage his less confident son to develop a more robust character, knowing full well the life he would have to lead.

Charles was taught from the earliest age of the high expectations and intense scrutiny that are the lot of an heir to the throne. Even as a small child, he was expected to make polite conversation and look people in the eye when speaking to them. Unlike his mother who had enjoyed 10 years of a relatively carefree childhood before knowing she would one day be Queen, his life as the future King of England was marked out from day one.

When George VI died on 6 February 1952, aged just 56, his 25-year-old daughter became Queen Elizabeth II and Charles, at just three years old, was now heir apparent. On his mother's accession, Prince Charles acquired six hereditary titles: Duke of Cornwall, Duke of Rothesay, Earl of Carrick, Baron of Renfrew, Lord of the Isles, and Prince and Great Steward of Scotland.

THE QUEEN'S CORONATION

Queen Elizabeth II ascended the throne during the greyest of Februarys. Her coronation was planned for the following June, allowing for a period of mourning, time for the preparations to take place, and with the hope for bright, warm weather.

One of Prince Charles' earliest memories is of being bathed by his nanny when his mother came into the nursery wearing St Edward's Crown, also known as the Coronation Crown. She was practising carrying its great weight – 4lbs 6oz (about 2kg) of solid gold – in preparation for the forthcoming ceremony, and her small son was transfixed by the glittering jewels.

Following months of anticipation, the coronation of Queen Elizabeth II took place on 2 June 1953 at Westminster Abbey. Unlike his young sister, Prince Charles, at four, was deemed old enough to attend the ceremony and received a special hand-painted invitation. He was dressed all in white for the occasion, and recalls being 'strapped into this outfit' of long trousers and a frilled shirt.

During the ceremony, Charles was photographed sitting in the royal gallery between the Queen Mother and Princess Margaret, head on hand, looking as bored as any child of his age might. However, at other times he appeared absorbed with the ritual and would turn to his grandmother to ask questions. In typical small boy mode, film footage also shows him wiping brilliantine from his hair then offering his sticky perfumed palm to her.

The BBC's televised coverage of the coronation was a milestone in the history of broadcasting. It was the first service to be televised and for many people it was the first time they had watched television.

Above: Prince Charles stands, head on hand, between the Queen Mother and Princess Margaret at Westminster Abbey to see his mother crowned Queen Elizabeth II.

The ceremony over, lunch was served in an annexe built in Westminster Abbey especially for the coronation. The Queen, dressed in her velvet robe and wearing the Imperial State Crown, then journeyed home in her coach, escorted by a Sovereign's Escort of the Household Cavalry.

Later, the Royal Family, Princess Anne included, gathered on the balcony of Buckingham Palace to wave to the crowds who had thronged to greet the newly crowned Queen. Although the weather had turned out to be dull and wet, it had not dampened the spirits of her subjects.

Left: Prince Charles and Princess Anne dressed in their Coronation Day outfits. Princess Anne wears a pearl necklace and ruby and diamond brooch belonging to her mother. The brooch was given to The Queen when she was a child by Queen Mary, her paternal grandmother.

Opposite page: The newly crowned Queen Elizabeth II, with her children standing alongside her, waves to the crowds outside Buckingham Palace as the Coronation entourage waits on the balcony to watch the fly-past of 168 jet planes – the Royal Air Force salute.

SCHOOLDAYS

On her accession, the new Queen and her family moved into Buckingham Palace. Shortly before Prince Charles turned five, a room in the nursery was converted into a classroom where he was schooled by governess Catherine Peebles. He was responsive to kindness and worked hard, although he did not display any of the intellectual curiosity that would define him in adulthood.

Shortly before his eighth birthday, it was deemed that Charles would benefit from the company of other children. When he started at Hill House School in Knightsbridge in November 1956, he was the first heir to the throne to attend school beyond royal walls. He settled quietly into school life, showing an aptitude in several subjects, including art – for which his report the following year recorded that he 'simply loves drawing and painting'.

In September 1957 Charles became a boarder at Cheam School in Hampshire. Prince Philip had attended Cheam at the same age, and as it had helped develop his own resilient character, he thought it would be ideal for his son. Charles, however, was terribly homesick and found it difficult to make friends. Fortunately, he had been taught to box and could defend himself in a tussle – but, as a result of such behaviour, on two occasions he was beaten by the headmaster. Charles took his punishment well, later saying: 'I am one of

Right: Prince Charles (second left) plays handball at Hill House School sports day, watched by his parents and sister.

those people for whom corporal punishment actually worked … I didn't do it again.'

Prince Philip also chose his son's secondary school: Gordonstoun, located in an isolated part of north-east Scotland. Established in 1934, Philip had been one of the first students at Gordonstoun where the motto was *Plus est en vous* (There is more in you). Although his father loved his time there, it was to be a very different story for 13-year-old Prince Charles, who later likened his ordeal to a 'prison sentence'.

The school had a 17th-century building at its centre, with prefabricated wooden huts – previously used as RAF barracks – for accommodation. The boys wore short trousers all year round, windows in the dormitories were open whatever the weather, and the school day began at 7.15am with a run and cold shower before breakfast.

Charles participated without complaint in all activities, including military-style assault courses, but found solace in pottery classes and classical music. Whilst at Cheam, he had demonstrated a talent for memorising excerpts from Shakespearian plays, and had felt at home on the stage. When a new English master, Eric Anderson, joined Gordonstoun in 1964, he encouraged the Prince to act in several Shakespeare dramas, casting him as the Duke of Exeter in *Henry V* and the lead in *Macbeth*.

Above: Prince Charles in his Cheam School uniform.

Prince Charles' happiest times during his latter school years were the two terms spent, at his father's suggestion, at Timbertop in a remote part of Victoria, Australia. Charles felt liberated by the informality of the country where he was not judged on his royal heritage and where students and masters treated him like one of them. He embraced the physical challenges with enthusiasm, undertaking cross-country expeditions of up to 70 miles over three days in relentless heat.

The Prince left Timbertop in July 1966; he returned to Gordonstoun for his final year that autumn and was appointed guardian (head boy). Having passed all six of his O levels two years previously, he was now studying A levels, and received a B in history and a C in French.

Charles left Gordonstoun with a greater steeliness and strength of purpose, but determined to look at different education options for any children he might have.

Right: Prince Charles in Sydney, Australia, in May 1966. He was spending two terms at Timbertop as part of his education, and made around 50 royal engagements in the country during that time.

CLOSE RELATIONS

With less than two years separating them, Princes Charles and Princess Anne (later the Princess Royal), confined to a sheltered childhood in the nursery and schoolroom of Buckingham Palace and a regime led by nannies and governesses, were inevitably close as they grew up.

Charles and Anne's paternal grandfather, Prince Andrew, fourth son of King George I of Greece, had died in 1944 and their grandmother, Princess Alice of Battenberg, was mainly absent from their lives. Their son, Prince Philip of Greece, had led a disrupted childhood, having been forced into exile with his parents and sisters in late 1922. Princess Alice suffered from mental health problems, which eventually led to a breakdown and her committal to a sanatorium. However, by the time Prince Charles was born she was fully recovered from her illness and living on the Greek island of Tinos, eventually becoming a nun. She wrote to Philip following the birth of his son: 'I think of you so much with a sweet baby of your own, of your joy and the interest you will take in all his little doings.'

Charles' closest relationship with a grandparent was with Queen Elizabeth the Queen Mother, who adored young children and was happy to indulge them. When his parents were away, he often visited her at Royal Lodge in Windsor Great Park. She gave the young Charles hugs, encouraged his kind and gentle nature, and introduced him to a world of

Charles' maternal great-grandmother, Queen Mary, died a few weeks before Queen Elizabeth II's coronation. Only four years old when his 'Gan-Gan' died, Charles had been the only child the formidable lady permitted to touch the precious collection of jade objects that she kept in locked cabinets.

Right: The Queen Mother hugs five-year-old Prince Charles as she leaves for a trip to the USA and Canada in 1954. Also in the photograph are Princess Anne, the Prime Minister Sir Winston Churchill and Princess Margaret.

Left: The Queen Mother and the Prince of Wales leave Sandringham Flower Show in July 2001, just days before her 101st birthday. The Queen Mother had been visiting the show regularly since before the Second World War.

music and art. They remained close throughout her long life and when she died, aged 101, on 30 March 2002 – just seven weeks after her younger daughter, Princess Margaret – it was a huge loss for Charles. Although he had seen his grandmother just two days before he set off for a long-planned skiing trip to Klosters, he minded desperately that he was not with her when she died. On 1 April he gave a moving tribute, broadcast from his home at Highgrove, in which he spoke of his grandmother's 'utterly irresistible mischievousness of spirit'; he reflected on how she had served the British people with 'panache, style and unswerving dignity', and said how much he would miss her laugh and 'wonderful wisdom born of so much experience and of an innate sensitivity to life'.

Particularly in the early years of her daughter's reign, the Queen Mother had filled a gap when Charles and Anne's parents were absent; the new Queen worked tirelessly, her royal duties having to take precedence over her young family. Queen Elizabeth II had been settled in her role as monarch for more than seven years when, in 1959, it was announced that she was expecting another child.

Right: The Queen and the Duke of Edinburgh's family was complete when Prince Edward was born in 1964. He was just over a year old when this photograph of him with his parents and siblings was taken at Frogmore in Windsor Home Park.

Prince Andrew Albert Christian Edward (later the Duke of York) was born on 19 February 1960. Four years later, on 10 March 1964, another son, The Queen and Duke of Edinburgh's last child, was born: Prince Edward Anthony Richard Louis (later the Earl of Wessex). The Queen was, by now, balancing work and family life and able to spend more time with her younger sons than she had her two elder children. Prince Charles and Princess Anne were already teenagers by the time Edward arrived and took delight in their much younger siblings. Just as he had doted on Anne, Charles loved his young brothers and would spend hours playing with them.

Perhaps the other biggest influence on the young Prince Charles' life was the man he saw as 'the grandfather he never had' – his great-uncle Lord Louis Mountbatten, the younger brother of Prince Philip's mother. The Admiral of the Fleet, Earl Mountbatten of Burma was also an important part of Prince Philip's life – and had been present at the Royal Naval College at Dartmouth in late July 1939 when the 13-year-old Princess Elizabeth met for the first time the handsome 18-year-old Prince Philip, who was on a three-month officers' training course.

Prince Charles was a regular visitor to Broadlands, the Hampshire home of Mountbatten and his wife, Edwina. Uncle Dickie, as the young Prince called him, was affectionate towards his great-nephew, and was adept at balancing criticism with praise. Charles found him easy to talk to and the older man often acted as a confidant to the Prince. Louis Mountbatten remained a constant in Charles' life and when he was killed by an IRA bomb as he piloted a boat out of the small seaside village of Mullaghmore in County Sligo in Northern Ireland on 27 August 1979, the Prince was unable to imagine how he would 'come to terms with the magnitude of such a deep loss'. Charles read the lesson at Lord Mountbatten's funeral, and at a memorial service in St Paul's Cathedral gave a 25-minute address during which he was unable to suppress his anger at the murder of his uncle and the other innocent victims killed in the terrorist attack.

Left: Prince Charles with Lord Mountbatten in 1954.

Left: This photograph of The Queen, the Duke of Edinburgh and their children was taken on board the royal yacht *Britannia* during a visit to Norway, and was used on Her Majesty's Christmas card in 1969.

In May 2015, Prince Charles made an historic visit to the Republic of Ireland and Northern Ireland. Central to the trip was his pilgrimage to Mullaghmore where Lord Louis Mountbatten had been killed. He met Timothy Knatchbull, who, with his parents, survived the 1979 IRA assassination that killed Timothy's twin brother Nicholas, who died alongside Lord Mountbatten and 15-year-old friend Paul Maxwell. Timothy's grandmother, the Dowager Baroness Brabourne, had died of her injuries the following day. Prince Charles expressed his hope that Britain and Ireland could forge 'a lasting legacy of peace, forgiveness and friendship' for future generations.

Left: The Duke and Duchess of Cornwall with Timothy Knatchbull in Ireland, May 2015.

19

UNIVERSITY YEARS

Prince Charles was the first heir to the throne to be enrolled for a university degree. The chosen university – Cambridge – was agreeable to the young man who admired its architectural glory and revered traditions. Another plus was its close proximity to the royal Sandringham Estate where he could indulge his passion for pheasant shoots and enjoy the comfort of Wood Farm farmhouse, which his mother permitted him to use, with its views looking out over the marshes to the North Sea.

Charles arrived at Trinity College, Cambridge in October 1967. A trip to Papua New Guinea whilst he was a student at Timbertop in Australia had stimulated an anthropological interest and, in a show of independence, he rejected the course of study chosen for him as future monarch, settling instead on one that combined anthropology and archaeology. He believed studying anthropology would prepare him for kingship, saying: 'If more people can be assisted to appreciate and understand their own social behaviour, the better and more healthy our society will be.'

The Prince's living quarters included accommodation for his detective and official equerry. Like all students, whatever their status, he was assigned a 'bedder' who would make his bed, tidy his room and serve him tea; unlike other students, though, Charles had the privilege of his own bathroom.

Just as at Cheam and Gordonstoun, with a few exceptions, the characteristically shy Charles found it difficult to make friends amongst his peers and instead found camaraderie outside the student body in the world of hunting and shooting that he knew and loved. Despite this being the 'Swinging Sixties', the Prince preferred to dress in the clothes in which he felt most comfortable: corduroy trousers and tweed jackets. With his hair neatly trimmed, he took pride in his conventional image and was 'happy to be square'.

Left: The student Prince: Charles cycling in Cambridge.

Whilst at Cambridge, Prince Charles was able to continue his enjoyment of acting, joining Trinity's drama group, the Dryden Society, in November 1968. Amongst other roles, he was cast in a comedy revue as a cleric and took a similar part in *The Erpingham Camp*, a dark comedy by Joe Orton.

The Prince had long taken pleasure in alternative comedy. As a child, a favourite book had been Hilaire Belloc's *Cautionary Tales for Children*, full of quirky characters. A big fan of BBC radio's *The Goon Show*, during his time at Timbertop Charles was known for his clever mimicry of its characters – in particular, Peter Sellers' 'Bluebottle'.

Above: Spike Milligan – who along with Harry Secombe, Peter Sellers and, at one time, Michael Bentine, starred in *The Goon Show* – receives an Honorary Knighthood from the Prince of Wales in 2002.

Charles was taking a keen interest in religion, influenced by the Revd Harry Williams, Dean of Chapel at Trinity, who introduced him to the works of Carl Jung and Sigmund Freud. Although Williams' teachings shocked fundamentalists, he and Charles dined together regularly, enjoying discussions that pushed the boundaries of traditional theology, and he said that the Prince had 'the grace, the humility and the desire to help other people'.

Mindful of his future role, in his second year Charles also studied history, including the British constitution. He was a conscientious student, considered talented by Master of Trinity Richard 'Rab' Butler; his Director of Studies reported that the student Prince wrote 'useful and thoughtful essays … he is interested in discussion and likes to draw parallels between the people we study and ourselves'. After three years' studying at Cambridge, Charles graduated on 23 June 1970 with a 2:2.

Right: The Prince of Wales graduated from Cambridge with a 2:2 in 1970, the first heir apparent to earn a university degree. He is seen here leaving Senate House, Cambridge in 1975, having been awarded a Master of Arts degree.

THE PRINCE OF WALES

*'And him Our most dear Son Charles Philip Arthur George as has been accustomed.
We do ennoble and invest with the said Principality and Earldom by girting him with
a Sword by putting a Coronet on his head and a Gold Ring on his finger and also by
delivering a Gold Rod in his hand.'*

With these noble words of the Letters Patent, The Queen created her son Prince of Wales in 1969. It was 11 years earlier, when Prince Charles was watching the closing ceremony of the Commonwealth Games in Cardiff on television with some school chums in the headmaster's study at Cheam, that he heard his mother declare in a recorded speech that he was to become the Prince of Wales. Attached to his new Welsh title would be yet another: Earl of Chester. Two weeks after the announcement, and en route to Scotland with his parents on the royal yacht *Britannia*, Charles visited Anglesey where he was warmly welcomed. His father put a comforting arm around his shoulder as they both waved to the crowds. But the boy was still only nine years old and it would be several years before he was invested as the 21st Prince of Wales.

The investiture was planned to take place on 1 July 1969, a few months before Prince Charles turned 21. It was to be held at the medieval Caernarfon Castle in north Wales, founded by King Edward I and where his son, Edward, the first Prince of Wales, was born in 1284.

In the lead-up to his investiture, the British public heard Prince Charles' voice – many for the first time – in a series of interviews on radio and television in which he came across as engaging, self-effacing and articulate.

In preparation for the ceremony, Charles was enrolled for a nine-week term at the University College of Wales at Aberystwyth, which exposed him to the Principality's language, history, culture and traditions. Several weeks before the end of term, he made his first speech in Welsh at a youth festival for poetry, drama and music, which earned him a standing ovation.

The Letters Patent read by The Queen and the insignia – the sword, coronet, mantle, gold ring and gold rod – were central to the ceremony. After Her Majesty had placed the jewelled coronet on Prince Charles' head to crown him Prince of Wales, she smoothed the mantle of purple velvet trimmed with ermine around his shoulders with a motherly touch. He then paid homage to her,

Below: Prince Charles' investiture as Prince of Wales at Caernarfon Castle.

Knight of the Garter

A full year before he was invested as Prince of Wales, on 17 June 1968 Prince Charles was invested and installed as a Knight of the Garter at St George's Chapel, Windsor.

Prince Charles' Garter robes are a mantle of deep blue, worn with a white-plumed cap. Blue has been the prescribed colour since King Edward III founded the Order in 1348. It was Edward III who appointed his son Edward, the second Prince of Wales and popularly known as the Black Prince, along with 24 other heroes of the French wars to be Founder-Knights; the King was Sovereign of the Order, bringing the total to 26.

The blue Garter, embroidered in gold with the motto *Honi soit qui mal y pense* (Shame be to him who thinks evil of it) is worn on the left leg, just below the knee, on certain ceremonial occasions. It is said to represent the garter belonging to Edward III's young cousin, Princess Joan of Kent, Countess of Salisbury, which fell to the floor whilst she was dancing at a royal ball in 1347. The King picked up the garter and silenced his courtiers with the reproof '*Honi soit qui mal y pense*', adding that it would soon be a symbol of supreme honour. The Princess later married the Black Prince in the chapel at Windsor where the earliest rites of the Order were celebrated annually on 23 April, St George's Day – St George being the patron saint of the Garter.

From the 18th century until 1946, appointments to the Order of the Garter, the world's oldest order of knighthood in continuous existence and the greatest British honour after the Victoria Cross and George Cross, were made on advice from the government. Since then the Order has returned to its original function as a mark of royal favour, with Knights of the Garter chosen by the sovereign to honour those who have given service of particular note to the sovereign or nation, including through holding public office. Although for much of its history the Garter was limited to the aristocracy, today Garter Knights come from a variety of backgrounds. Membership remains limited, consisting of the reigning sovereign, the Prince of Wales – both being members by virtue of status and gaining membership upon acceding to one of the titles – and 24 full members (known as a Knights Companion or Ladies Companion). The Order can also include certain additional members of the Royal Family and foreign monarchs.

Although the sovereign still announces new Knights of the Garter on St George's Day, today they are invested and installed on the Monday of Royal Ascot week. After receiving the insignia from Her Majesty, a Knight elect processes with all the other Garter Knights, including The Queen and the Duke of Edinburgh, through the grounds of Windsor Castle to a service of installation at St George's Chapel.

Above: Prince Charles and the Queen Mother process during the Knights of the Garter ceremony at Windsor in June 1969, just days before his investiture as Prince of Wales.

which he later recalled as being the most moving moment for him: as The Queen placed her hands between his, he declared to be her 'liege man of life and limb and of earthly worship… to live and die against all manner of folks'.

Charles carried off the whole event with great composure, including speeches that he made in both English and Welsh which were followed by a short religious service. In the meantime, throughout the country children were enjoying street parties in celebration of the occasion. Following his investiture, the Prince made a three-day tour of Wales, and was touched by the support of the Welsh people everywhere he went.

His Royal Highness Prince Charles holds a number of titles. As well as Prince of Wales he is: Knight of the Garter (KG); Knight of the Thistle (KT); Knight Grand Cross of the Order of the Bath (KGCB); Order of Merit (OM); Knight of the Order of Australia (AK); Companion of the Queen's Service Order (QSO); Privy Counsellor (PC); Aide-de-Camp (ADC); Earl of Chester; Duke of Cornwall; Duke of Rothesay; Earl of Carrick; Baron of Renfrew; Lord of the Isles; Prince and Great Steward of Scotland. Some titles are used, depending on where His Royal Highness is in the United Kingdom; for example, when in Scotland he is known as the Duke of Rothesay, a title first given by Robert III, King of Scots, to his son David in 1398.

The symbol of the Prince of Wales' Feathers was first used in the 14th century by the Black Prince. The badge comprises three feathers rising behind a gold coronet decorated with crosses and fleur-de-lys, and the motto *Ich Dien* (I serve) depicted on dark blue ribbon. There are various theories about how the symbol and motto came into being: one suggests the feathers were used by the family of the Black Prince's mother, Philippa of Hainault, and that the motto formed part of the arms of the King of Bohemia. Along with The Queen and the Duke of Edinburgh, the Prince of Wales can grant Royal Warrants of appointment to a company. Those approved by the Prince are entitled to display the Prince of Wales' Feathers on their products. The history of the Royal Warrant dates back to medieval times when competition for royal favour was intense and the monarch had the pick of the country's best tradespeople.

The Prince of Wales also has a coat of arms with historical links to the heraldry of his ancestors. The main shield is the Royal Arms of the United Kingdom, used in its current form since Queen Victoria was sovereign. The first and fourth quarters represent England, with three gold lions on a red background; the second quarter has Scotland's red lion rampant on gold, and the third quarter depicts the golden harp of Ireland on a blue background. Prince Charles also has three standards: his Personal Standard and Standards for Scotland and Wales. They are used depending on where he is in the United Kingdom, with rules governing their use.

The Personal Standard is the same as the Standard used by previous Princes of Wales. The banner includes the Royal Arms, the Coronet of the Heir Apparent, and the Arms of the Principality of Wales. It was Charles, the Prince of Wales himself, who had the idea of incorporating his Scottish titles into a banner; used exclusively when he is Scotland, it was first flown on 21 July 1976. The Duke of Edinburgh suggested that the Prince of Wales have his own flag to use during visits to Wales. It is based on the Arms of the Principality of Wales once borne by Llywelyn the Great and Llywelyn ap Gruffudd, last native Princes of Wales. The flag was first flown on 11 June 1969, three weeks before Prince Charles was invested as Prince of Wales.

Above: Prince Charles kneels before his mother during his investiture ceremony, 1 July 1969.

The investiture was two years in the planning, tailored for broadcast on colour television – still a fairly new phenomenon in Britain – under the direction of Lord Snowdon, Charles' uncle and husband of Princess Margaret. What was seen as Prince Charles' official 'coming of age' was watched by 500 million worldwide.

A CAREER IN THE ARMED FORCES

Both the Duke of Edinburgh and Lord Mountbatten were keen for Prince Charles to follow in their footsteps and those of both of his great-grandfathers by attending the Royal Naval College, Dartmouth, and serving as a naval officer.

However, in March 1971 the Prince of Wales first started his career in the services at RAF Cranwell in Lincolnshire. A year's training was compressed into five months, and he applied himself well to every task. He had already taken flying lessons during his second year at Cambridge and had flown solo for the first time in 1969, so learning to fly jets was a natural progression and one that he loved. He received his wings on 20 August 1971 having enjoyed his time amongst the officers who had made him feel so welcome.

Right: Prince Charles piloting a fighter jet.

Charles started at the Royal Naval College, Dartmouth the following month. Again, his training was condensed from the customary three months to six weeks. He flew to Gibraltar on 5 November to join the destroyer HMS *Norfolk*, spending seven months at sea living in a small cabin. From May 1972 he spent six months on land studying at various naval schools before setting off in January 1973 on HMS *Minerva*, a smaller destroyer with fewer officers, which meant greater responsibilities for junior naval officer Prince Charles.

January 1974 saw him join HMS *Jupiter* in Singapore as the ship's communication officer. He was also in charge of 15 non-commissioned officers. During his time at Timbertop in Australia, the headmaster Thomas

Left: The Queen, Lord High Admiral of the United Kingdom 1964–2011, is piped aboard HMS *Bronington*. She was visiting the ship's commander, her son Prince Charles (far right), on his 28th birthday.

In July 1971, during his time in the RAF, Prince Charles made his first parachute jump – and it could easily have ended in tragedy. He had no hesitation in jumping from the plane when his turn came – but as he tumbled out of the slipstream and his parachute opened he found himself upside down, his feet tangled in the rigging. He kept calm and was able to untangle himself before touching down on the waters of Studland Bay in Dorset. After the experience, he joked that he had only had a 'short time to admire the view'.

Six years later he enlisted on a parachute course after being appointed Colonel-in-Chief of the Parachute Regiment, saying: 'I didn't think I could look them in the eye or indeed ever dream of wearing the beret with the Parachute Regiment badge unless I'd done the course.'

Garnett had reported that Charles proved an admirable leader when put in charge of younger students; his role on *Jupiter* played to this strength and he handled his men's professional and personal problems extremely well.

In July of that year, the Prince was frustrated when the Ministry of Defence decided against sending him into a war zone when conflict broke out between Greece and Turkey. However, he was granted permission to train as a helicopter pilot that autumn and told that he could join the commando carrier HMS *Hermes* to fly helicopters in spring 1975. A keen pilot and a quick learner, he became a qualified helicopter pilot in December 1974, and left England for HMS *Hermes* the following March.

For Prince Charles' final tour of duty in the Royal Navy, he was given command of coastal minesweeper HMS *Bronington* in February 1976. Once more, his people skills came to the fore and morale was high amongst his men. When he left the Navy in December that year, he had attained an 'excellent level of professional competence'.

The Prince of Wales has been involved with the armed services ever since, and serving for five years has given him credence when he wears the uniforms of regiments around the world that he oversees as honorary Colonel-in-Chief.

Above: Prince Charles, Colonel-in-Chief of the Parachute Regiment, chats to a young recruit at the Airborne Forces Day parade in Aldershot in 1978.

Left: The Prince of Wales at the controls of a Wessex helicopter in December 1974. He was taking off to lead a massed flypast of helicopters of 707 Squadron at Royal Naval Air Station Yeovilton, Somerset, who were celebrating their 10th anniversary.

A YOUNG ROYAL AMBASSADOR

As he approached his 21st birthday, Prince Charles was asked to describe the moment he first realised he was heir to the throne. He responded: 'I think it's something that dawns on you with the most ghastly inexorable sense… and slowly you get the idea that you have a certain duty and responsibility.'

Even as a child, Charles had lived with the knowledge of duty and obligation that comes with the territory of being heir apparent. Soon after his 18th birthday, the Prince was named Counsellor of State. Other Counsellors of State then included the Duke of Edinburgh, the Queen Mother, Princess Margaret and Prince Henry Duke of Gloucester, and it was a role that empowered him to act on The Queen's behalf when she was out of the country and would enable him to become Prince Regent if she became incapacitated. Today's Counsellors of State are the Duke of Edinburgh, Prince Charles, Prince Andrew, Prince William and Prince Harry.

Shortly after going up to Cambridge, in October 1967 Charles attended his first State Opening of Parliament, presided over by his mother. Two months later he represented The Queen for the first time overseas at the funeral of the Prime Minister of Australia, Harold Holt. It was a country that he felt a great affinity with since his time at Timbertop when he attended around 50 official engagements, his first solo experience of representing the

Right: Both Prince Charles and Princess Anne attended their first State Opening of Parliament in 1967.

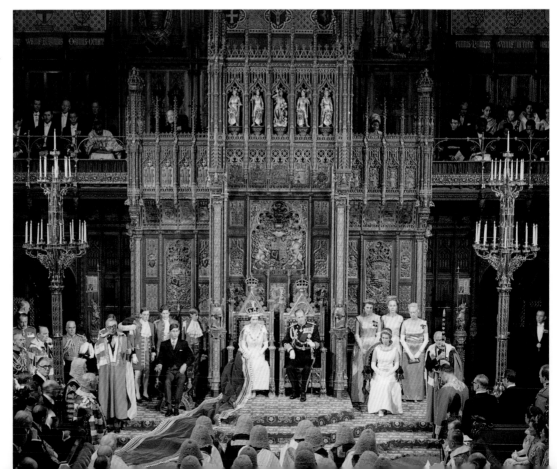

Above: The Prince of Wales, his sister and father, follow The Queen and American President Richard Nixon as they walk through Buckingham Palace in 1969. It was Mr Nixon's first official visit to the United Kingdom as President of the USA.

Above: Prince Charles first fell in love with Fiji in 1970. He is seen here being warmly welcomed on a return visit in 2005, his fourth time in the country.

Royal Family in this way. That first Australian experience had given the shy young man confidence to take the plunge and engage with people; it turned out to be a very positive experience, which he said 'suddenly unlocked a completely different feeling, and I was then able to communicate and talk to people so much more'. That new-found confidence was perhaps even more remarkable as, other than his time at Timbertop, it was one of few occasions that he'd left Europe, his first being aged five when he and Princess Anne had travelled to Libya and Malta at the end of their parents' Commonwealth tour in 1954.

Summer 1968 saw Charles making his inaugural official foreign visit to Malta, and he spent time shadowing public service employees at several government departments in London to gain an understanding of their jobs.

The Prince of Wales was taken out of university for four weeks in the spring of 1970 for a royal tour of Australia, Hong Kong, New Zealand and Japan, his route taking him to the USA for the first time. In July that year, he and Princess Anne took centre stage on a three-day visit to the White House as guests of President Nixon. In October 1970, Prince Charles represented The Queen at the independence celebrations in the former British colony of Fiji, where he admired the gentle people who had 'the most perfect and touching manners and the greatest dignity and humour I have ever seen'.

Thus the Prince was already a talented diplomat and familiar with performing royal duties when he made the transition into civilian life in 1977, The Queen's Silver Jubilee year. He had a strong desire to shape his life into one that would be fulfilling whilst he bided his time until he accedes to the throne. Shortly before his 30th birthday in November 1978, during a lecture at Cambridge Union Society, he revealed, 'My great problem in life is that I do not really know what my role in life is. At the moment I do not have one. But somehow I must find one.'

A SPORTING PRINCE

Queen Elizabeth II has always had a passion for everything equestrian, and it was she who taught Prince Charles to ride when he was four. Although initially timid on horseback, he was soon at home in the saddle, although – unlike his bolder sister – he feared jumping. This was an anxiety he overcame in the mid-1970s when, having decided he wanted to hunt, he took lessons – including from Princess Anne. Charles first hunted at Badminton with the Beaufort Hunt in February 1975 and was immediately hooked.

Eager to follow his father's lead, the Prince took up polo at the age of 12. By 1964, under the Duke of Edinburgh's watchful eye, the teenager was applying himself well to the sport. A few years later, Charles joined the polo team at Cambridge; a tough and passionate player, he competed at the highest level and won a half blue.

The Duke of Edinburgh also taught a young Prince Charles to swim, shoot and fish, and the latter in particular was an occupation he enjoyed with his grandmother. Charles also became a competent sailor as a youngster, regularly taking to the water at Cowes with his father's friend, the boat designer and sailing enthusiast Uffa Fox.

In early 1977 the Prince of Wales added to his sporting prowess during his first stay at Klosters in Switzerland at the invitation of friends Charles and Patti Palmer-Tomkinson. Just as he rode ponies to the limit on the polo field and horses in the same way when hunting, he proved to be fearless on the ski slopes and was soon skiing off-piste. An annual trip to Klosters became a fixture on the royal calendar.

Below left:
The Queen and Prince Charles riding at Windsor in 1961.

Below right:
The Prince of Wales at a Household Brigade Polo Club match, Smith's Lawn, Windsor Great Park, in 1965.

The Hunting Act 2004 came into effect on 18 February 2005 and the previous day Prince Charles had ridden out with the hunt for the last time. It was the same year that he hung up his polo mallet. Polo had been an important part of his psychological and physical wellbeing for many decades. It was a sport he enjoyed with his sons and, despite his advisors trying to persuade him to retire after numerous bones had been broken, it was not until 2005 when his back was proving too painful that he made the decision for himself, handing over his polo ponies to his sons who continue the royal tradition of fund-raising through various charity polo matches.

Nevertheless, the Prince of Wales still participates in shooting and hiking with a vigour that can leave friends half his age trailing in his wake. Like his mother, Prince Charles loves dogs, and one is rarely far from his heel when he is out in the countryside.

In 1988 a terrible skiing incident nearly cost Prince Charles his life. He was enjoying a holiday at Klosters with family and friends – including the Palmer-Tomkinsons and Major Hugh Lindsay, former equerry to The Queen – when some of the party decided to go for one final run of the day, led by local guide Bruno Sprecher. No one could have predicted the events that were to follow. An avalanche hurtled down the mountain; Sprecher shouted 'Jump!' and Prince Charles and Charles Palmer-Tomkinson made it onto a ledge next to the rock face, but the wall of snow swept Hugh Lindsay and Patti Palmer-Tomkinson over the edge. Patti was critically injured but Hugh Lindsay was killed. His wife, Sarah Lindsay, gave birth to their first child two months later, and, whilst others shied away, Prince Charles made sure he was available to her and encouraged her to talk of her husband as often as she wanted and needed to.

Left: Princes William and Harry with their father on a skiing holiday in Klosters, Switzerland in 2002.

PRINCELY PASTIMES

Despite his 'man of action' image, out of the sporting arena Prince Charles has always demonstrated a love of more gentle pursuits.

During the summer before his final year at Cambridge, Charles wrote his first book whilst on holiday with his family in the Western Isles aboard the royal yacht *Britannia*. It was a story he invented to entertain his young brothers, Andrew and Edward, which tells of an old man who lives in a cave under Lochnagar, a mountain overlooking the royal estate at Balmoral. *The Old Man of Lochnagar* was published more than a decade later in aid of one of Charles' charities, The Prince's Trust.

It was the Queen Mother who instilled and encouraged Charles' love and talent for art, a subject for which he was praised in school reports. Between leaving university and starting his career in the armed forces, he took up watercolour painting and was further encouraged in his artistic endeavours by his father, a keen oil painter.

Charles greatly admires the work of 18th-century artist J.M.W. Turner. Landscapes became the Prince's preferred medium as an outlet for creative expression and he was 'exhilarated at being transported into another dimension' with his pictures that display a delicate intimacy, coupled with a sense of melancholy. Although he enjoys painting in the open air it is not always possible, so he makes a habit of drawing rough sketches and making notes about the colours, the light and so forth, then paints the landscape in his studio,

Right: Prince Charles, who as an artist uses the name A.G. Carrick, with one of his watercolours of the Castle of Mey. The pseudonym is formed from two of the Prince's Christian names – Arthur and George – and one of his titles, Earl of Carrick.

Left: The Prince
of Wales with
members of the
Welsh National
Opera at their 70th
anniversary gala
concert which was
held in Buckingham
Palace in 2016. The
Prince not only
enjoys listening to
music but is himself
an accomplished
cellist.

when his busy schedule allows. A gratifying personal achievement has been the commercial success of his artworks, which have raised millions of pounds for his charities.

It was also his grandmother who instilled a love of music in the young Charles. Although classical music may have been common ground between them, rock and pop music have long been an important part of the Prince's life. Many famous stars of the music industry support The Prince's Trust; the first benefit gig for the charity took place in July 1982 at the Dominion Theatre in London. With such names as Pete Townshend, Phil Collins, Jethro Tull and Kate Bush headlining, it was a sellout.

With music, of course, comes dancing, and Prince Charles has always been an enthusiastic and uncharacteristically uninhibited dancer. He had private lessons from Madame Betty Vacani at Buckingham Palace and prides himself on his prowess on the ballroom floor.

In 1988 Prince Charles chose to mark his 40th birthday by celebrating with 1,500 young people who had been helped by The Prince's Trust. At this daytime party, he danced with several of the partygoers, one of whom said, 'He dances well for an old man!' That evening a black tie ball for 300 guests was hosted in their son's honour by The Queen and Prince Philip at Buckingham Palace. After the formalities, two rooms were set aside for dancing – one ballroom, the other disco.

The Queen Mother loved to hold parties at Birkhall on the Balmoral Estate. These would often involve dancing Scottish reels in which she encouraged a young Prince Charles to participate with eligible debutantes. In September 2001, six months before she died, Charles had cancelled a holiday to fly to Birkhall to join his grandmother. Although she had turned 101 the previous month, one evening she felt perky enough to dance a Highland reel. Nevertheless, as her biographer William Shawcross observed, 'there was an elegiac note' to her mood and her grandson knew he faced the unspoken reality of her final decline.

Below: Prince
Charles partners a
young woman on
the dance floor at
one of the parties
to celebrate his
40th birthday. This
particular celebration
was held at the
Aston Manor Road
Transport Museum
in Birmingham,
transformed from
a derelict tram
shed, which he had
formally opened
that day.

AN ELIGIBLE BACHELOR

The heir to the throne was an eminently eligible bachelor and the tabloids had a field day speculating on any young lady who appeared to catch his eye. Amongst them, but not exclusively so, were members of the aristocracy.

At university in 1969, Rab Butler introduced Charles to Lucia Santa Cruz, daughter of the Chilean ambassador to Britain. She was working for the Master of Trinity as a research assistant on his memoirs. It has been claimed that she was the 'first love of his life', but a permanent relationship was out of the question: Lucia was Roman Catholic and the heir to the throne was, at that time, required by law to marry a Protestant. However, to this day they remain good friends, and it was she who first introduced him to the woman who was to have a huge impact on his life: Camilla Shand.

It is a popular misconception that Charles and Camilla first met at a polo match at Smith's Lawn; they met in the summer of 1972 through their mutual friend Lucia Santa Cruz who lived in the same block of flats as Camilla. Charles, who was between postings on HMS *Norfolk* and HMS *Minerva*, was immediately smitten by the warm, unassuming 25-year-old who shared his love of the countryside, his sense of humour and his indifference to the latest fashions.

Despite their mutual attraction, Prince Charles was still only 24 and not yet ready to settle down. Camilla was in a long-term on-off relationship with the handsome Andrew Parker Bowles, a one-time boyfriend of Princess Anne. Charles and Camilla became the greatest of friends and on hearing the news of her engagement to Parker Bowles in March 1973, the Prince, on board HMS *Minerva* in the West Indies, was bereft. Charles did not attend Andrew and Camilla's wedding four months later, claiming he was duty-bound to attend Independence Day celebrations elsewhere, but he was godfather to their first child, Tom.

When Princess Anne married Captain Mark Phillips in November 1973, there was a fresh round of conjecture about her elder brother's marriage prospects and the press was paying close attention to Charles' relationship with Lady Jane Wellesley, the 22-year-old daughter of the Duke of Wellington, but any romance there may have been fizzled out.

Below: The Prince of Wales with Lucia Santa Cruz following a theatre trip in 1970.

Left: Prince Charles, photographed shortly before his 30th birthday, with his Labrador, Harvey, at Balmoral. The Prince is wearing a kilt of Hunting Stewart tartan which once belonged to his grandfather, King George VI.

Above: The Queen's Procession arrives in Westminster Abbey for the wedding of Princess Anne and Captain Mark Phillips on 14 November 1973. The uniformed Prince of Wales walks behind his mother and grandmother and beside his brother, Prince Andrew. The wedding took place on Prince Charles' 25th birthday and fuelled speculation about who would one day be his bride.

'Uncle Dickie' thought his granddaughter Amanda Knatchbull would make Charles the perfect wife; she fitted Mountbatten's recommendation that the Prince find a 'suitable and sweet charactered girl before she met anyone else she might fall for'. But as second cousins they had known each other since childhood, and a long-term romance was not to be.

In June 1977 he met Lady Sarah Spencer, daughter of the 8th Earl Spencer, at a house party at Windsor Castle. Charles was invited to Sarah's home, Althorp, where he first met her younger sister, 16-year-old Diana. Both girls were invited to the Prince's 30th birthday party at Buckingham Palace the following year.

Despite rising pressure on Prince Charles to choose a bride, he was increasingly concerned that whoever he married would suffer 'an immense sacrifice and a great loss of freedom'.

DIANA, PRINCESS OF WALES

Lady Diana Spencer matched perfectly Lord Mountbatten's vision for Charles to take as a bride a 'sweet charactered girl' without a romantic past.

The Prince's romance with Diana started at Balmoral in the summer of 1980, whilst he was on holiday and she was helping her sister Jane – married to Robert Fellowes, assistant private secretary to The Queen – to care for the Fellowes' new-born child. The Queen approved of Charles' friendship with the 19-year-old, inviting her to the Braemar Gathering that autumn. The press was soon hounding demure 'shy Di', as they nicknamed Diana, and the world speculated about whether the Prince of Wales would propose to this young kindergarten assistant.

Despite their short courtship and his uncertainty about their relationship, Prince Charles asked Lady Diana for her hand and their engagement was announced in February 1981. Diana's life changed immediately. Having enjoyed the freedom of flat-sharing with friends, she was moved to royal quarters to protect her from the spotlight as wedding plans took shape and she was instructed in the demanding duties expected of a future Queen.

The nation was whipped into a frenzy of excitement for the royal wedding that took place on 29 July 1981 at St Paul's Cathedral. There were 2,500 wedding guests at St Paul's; the groom wore the full-dress uniform of a naval commander and the bride a beautiful ivory silk taffeta gown designed by David and Elizabeth Emanuel. The televised wedding ceremony, officiated by Archbishop of Canterbury Robert Runcie who proclaimed it 'the stuff of which fairytales are made', was seen around the world by 750 million people.

Below: Prince Charles and Lady Diana Spencer were engaged on 24 February 1981.

Back at Buckingham Palace for the wedding breakfast, the Royal Family made its customary appearance on the balcony and the crowds cheered when Charles kissed the new Princess of Wales. Later, an open landau carried them to Waterloo Station and they travelled to Broadlands to begin their honeymoon, just as Charles' parents had done nearly 34 years earlier.

That Charles and Diana's marriage ended unhappily has been well documented. However, what has never been in doubt is the joy that the birth of their two sons, Prince William and Prince Harry, brought the couple and thus the blessing of their union cannot be denied.

Left: The Prince and Princess of Wales at Buckingham Palace after their wedding at St Paul's Cathedral, 29 July 1981. Their wedding day was made a public holiday and there were celebrations throughout the land.

Below: Prince Charles accompanied the coffin bearing the body of Diana, Princess of Wales on the aircraft which flew from Paris to RAF Northolt. Her coffin, draped in the Royal Standard, was carried in a slow march across the tarmac by airmen of the Royal Air Force. The nation was united in grief for the Princess' royal ceremonial funeral which took place on 6 September 1997.

Prince Charles wanted a special memento of his and Diana's wedding, and commissioned watercolour artist John Ward to sit in the choir of St Paul's and create a painting of the ceremony.

When Prime Minister John Major announced the Prince and Princess of Wales' separation in December 1992, the couple's united message was that they were both intent on continuing to provide 'a happy and secure upbringing' for their sons.

Charles and Diana had been divorced for just a year when she was killed in a car crash in Paris on 31 August 1997. Despite their differences, Charles still held Diana in deep affection; distressed beyond measure and worried about his sons, he flew to Paris, accompanied by the Princess' sisters, Sarah and Jane, to bring her body home.

The Queen, at Balmoral when news of Diana's death broke, was criticised by the media for not making an official announcement or returning to London immediately. However, her priority was her grandsons, and she consoled them in private. Above all she wanted to protect them from the public eye for as long as possible.

Following the funeral, Diana, Princess of Wales was laid to rest on an island at her family home, the Althorp Estate in Northamptonshire.

PRINCE WILLIAM

Above: The Prince and Princess of Wales leave hospital with their new-born son Prince William.

In October 1981, just three months after their wedding, the Prince and Princess of Wales were overjoyed to learn that she was pregnant with their first child. 'Baby Wales' was born on 21 June 1982, the first heir to the throne to be delivered in hospital rather than a royal palace. Well-wishers and journalists gathered outside St Mary's Hospital, Paddington when, two days later, the 33-year-old Prince of Wales and his wife – still eight days shy of her 21st birthday – introduced their baby to the world. Before the family drove home to Kensington Palace, Prince Charles spoke of the pleasure the birth of their son had given him and Diana, adding: 'It has made me incredibly proud and somewhat amazed.'

Prince William Arthur Philip Louis of Wales was christened on 4 August. Charles and Diana were hands-on parents, and Charles made sure he spent as much time as he could with his son. In a break with royal tradition, when Charles and Diana travelled to Australia for a royal tour the following spring, William went with them.

The Prince and Princess of Wales were determined to make the childhoods of William and his younger brother, Prince Harry – born two years later – as normal as possible. At the age of three, William went to nursery school where he learned to socialise with other children. Two years later he went to Wetherby School in Notting Hill, then boarded at Ludgrove School in Berkshire before starting at Eton College in September 1995.

Despite Charles and Diana's eventual separation, their sons knew how much both parents loved them, and the boys in turn adored their parents. When their mother died in 1997 they were, quite naturally, devastated. In public William and Harry, just 15 and 12 respectively, kept their emotions under control with a maturity beyond their tender years. Secure in his home life with his father and brother, and with his grandmother, The Queen, providing what William later called 'a strong female influence' who did not hesitate to discipline him when necessary, William continued to do well at school. After A levels he took a gap year before going up to St Andrews University in Scotland where he would meet the girl who would one day become his wife.

Catherine Middleton, born into an ordinary, close-knit, middle-class family in January 1982, was the best of friends with Prince William for over a year before their relationship blossomed. Catherine was popular with the rest of the Royal Family and coped admirably with the often over-zealous attention of the press.

On their marriage, William and Catherine received three new titles: Duke and Duchess of Cambridge, Earl and Countess of Strathearn, and Baron and Baroness Carrickfergus.

Above: The Duke and Duchess of Cambridge on the balcony at Buckingham Palace following their wedding at Westminster Abbey.

Although, like his father before him, Prince William could have had his pick of European princesses and aristocratic young women, in November 2010 he and Catherine – clearly very much in love – became engaged. William presented his bride-to-be with an engagement ring that held special memories: the beautiful sapphire surrounded by 14 brilliant-cut diamonds and set in a white-gold band was the one that Prince Charles had given to William's mother, Princess Diana, on their engagement.

When William and Catherine married at Westminster Abbey on 29 April 2011, thousands of people throughout Britain celebrated and millions more around the world watched this happiest of royal occasions on television.

Left: Prince Charles and his sons pose for photographers at Klosters in Switzerland in 2000.

PRINCE HARRY

Charles and Diana could not have been more thrilled at the birth of a second son, Henry Charles Albert David (always known as Harry) on 15 September 1984. They now had 'an heir and a spare', although at this time, had their first child been a girl, the Succession to the Crown Act would have dictated Harry as heir to the throne after Charles.

Prince Charles was fascinated by his sons' different characters. Harry was a more placid child than his boisterous big brother, but the two were soon playmates and good friends. From an early age, their father shared his love of the countryside with the boys and taught them to hunt, shoot and fish.

Schooldays saw Harry following in William's footsteps to nursery school, Wetherby, Ludgrove and Eton. Their father was conscientious about turning up for parents' meetings and was an easy conversationalist with other children and their parents. Both William and Harry were popular with their peers and excelled at sport, including polo – another activity which, along with skiing, they were able to enjoy with their father.

After completing his A levels, Harry took a gap year, working in a cattle station in Australia and with orphaned children in Lesotho. He then joined the Royal Military Academy at Sandhurst in May 2005, passing out in April 2006. This time William followed in his younger brother's footsteps, joining RMA Sandhurst in January 2006 and passing out in December that year before training in the Royal Navy and RAF. After receiving his wings in 2008, William served as a helicopter pilot, first with RAF Search and Rescue and then with the East Anglian Air Ambulance.

Harry, meanwhile, spent 10 years in the armed forces. He trained as an Apache helicopter pilot and was twice deployed on tours of duty to Afghanistan; as a co-pilot gunner,

Below left: Four generations: a formal family portrait following the christening of Prince Harry which took place on 21 December 1984.

Below right: Prince Harry and big brother Prince William wave to photographers as they arrive with their parents for Harry's first day at Mrs Mynor's nursery school in Notting Hill in September 1987.

In the 1950s the Royal Family was not accustomed to giving public displays of affection, and there is a famous photograph of The Queen returning from a Commonwealth tour in 1952 and greeting four-year-old Prince Charles with a formal handshake. The image was in sharp contrast to a photograph taken in 1991 when the Prince and Princess of Wales, on a tour of Canada with their children, returned after a day of engagements to the royal yacht *Britannia*. Diana, arms outstretched, scooped William and Harry into a bear hug; those who witnessed the scene at close range also saw Charles bend down and give the boys more restrained but equally warm kisses and cuddles.

Right: Prince Harry, just returned from Afghanistan, leaves the terminal at RAF Brize Norton with his father and brother. The date is 1 March 2008 – St David's Day – and the Prince of Wales wears a leek, the national symbol of Wales, in his lapel.

he participated in at least one Hellfire missile attack on the Taliban. Prince Charles was proud of his son's bravery but confessed to anxiety in not knowing Harry's whereabouts.

Prince Harry ended his operational duties in 2015 and Prince William finished his employment as a helicopter pilot in summer 2017. Both are now full-time royals, supporting their grandmother and father in royal duties.

Before leaving the forces, Harry vowed to work to support service personnel who have been injured, physically and/or mentally. One of his initiatives has been the Invictus Games, an international adaptive sporting event for wounded, injured and sick servicemen and women, both serving and veterans. The first games were held in London in 2014. Mental health is a subject close to William and Harry's hearts; in 2017 they both spoke of how they had suffered by keeping a 'stiff upper lip' following their mother's death in 1997.

Left: There is a very close bond between Prince Charles and his sons, who are seen sharing a joke during day two of the Invictus Games at Lee Valley Athletics Centre, London in 2014.

CAMILLA, DUCHESS OF CORNWALL

Camilla Rosemary Shand was born on 17 July 1947 at King's College Hospital in London, delivered by the same obstetrician who would deliver Prince Charles the following year. Hers was a happy childhood growing up in East Sussex where she and her younger siblings enjoyed the countryside, with days spent picnicking, camping, walking dogs and horse riding. Pony-mad Camilla rode with the hunt from the age of nine, and it was eventually to become a hobby that she and Prince Charles enjoyed together. Camilla first met the man who was to become her first husband, Andrew Parker Bowles, in 1966. They had two children together, Tom and Laura, but it was not the happiest of marriages. After their divorce in 1995, Camilla set up a new family home for her and her children, Ray Mill House in Wiltshire.

Ever since they first met in 1972, Camilla was someone Charles could turn to, knowing that anything he discussed with her would be treated with complete confidentiality. She was to become the person who helped him through dark moments of self-doubt and despair.

After Diana's death, Charles and Camilla started to bring their burgeoning relationship out of the shadows, and in December 1997 Charles, William and Harry took part in a hunt at which Mrs Parker Bowles was also present. Charles and Camilla were first photographed together as a couple in January 1999 as they left the Ritz Hotel in Piccadilly following a party for Camilla's sister, Annabel.

It is said that The Queen did not initially approve of the relationship, but her son was not going to negotiate: he was determined to spend the rest of his life with the woman he loves. In 2000 his mother relented and met Camilla, briefly, at a 60th birthday party hosted by Charles that June for his cousin, the ex-King Constantine of Greece, grandson of Prince Philip's uncle.

On 10 February 2005, Clarence House announced the Prince of Wales and Camilla Parker Bowles were engaged. Charles' formal request to The Queen before proposing was a requirement of the Royal Marriages Act of 1772. Charles presented his bride-to-be with a platinum and diamond ring that had once belonged to the Queen Mother. Princes William and Harry were told of the engagement some weeks previously and when the news became public issued a joint statement expressing their happiness for their father and Camilla.

Below: Their first public embrace: the Prince of Wales is greeted by Camilla Parker Bowles as he arrives at Somerset House, London for the 15th anniversary reception for the National Osteoporosis Society in 2001.

The question of Prince Charles marrying Camilla Parker Bowles raised constitutional issues for both the Church of England and the monarchy. When he becomes King, Charles will become Supreme Governor of the Church; church rules on the remarriage of divorcees are complicated, but as early as 1998 the Bishop of Durham said there was no reason why Charles could not remarry and still maintain the moral authority to become Head of the Church.

Left: The Prince of Wales and his bride Camilla, Duchess of Cornwall in the White Drawing Room at Windsor Castle on their wedding day.

When Charles and Camilla married on 9 April 2005, she became Duchess of Cornwall – only the third woman in history to bear that title, the others being the wife of King George II, Caroline of Ansbach, and King George V's wife, Mary of Teck – Prince Charles' maternal great-grandmother.

There were two ceremonies, both joyous affairs. The civil ceremony took place in Windsor Guildhall. Although The Queen and Prince Philip were not at that ceremony, they did attend the service of prayer and dedication that followed, led by the Archbishop of Canterbury in St George's Chapel. At a reception later that day, The Queen spoke of her pride in the couple, happy in the knowledge that her son was 'home and dry with the woman he loves'.

The Duchess of Cornwall has become patron or president to a number of charities since her marriage to the Prince of Wales, but even before that she was involved with the National Osteoporosis Society. It is a charity close to her heart as her mother, Rosalind Shand, and grandmother, Sonia Keppell, both died of the disease. Camilla has supported the charity since 1994, became a patron in 1997 and president in 2001.

Above: Charles and Camilla, the Duke and Duchess of Rothesay, were on honeymoon when they undertook their first joint official engagement, the opening of Monaltrie Park children's playground in Ballater, near Balmoral, on 14 April 2005.

A PROUD GRANDFATHER

The birth of William and Catherine's first child, George Alexander Louis, on 22 July 2013 meant that for the first time since the reign of Queen Victoria, when her great-grandson – the future King Edward VIII – was born in 1894, the monarchy had three generations of heirs to the throne.

Of all the responses to the news of the latest addition to the Royal Family, one of the most heartfelt was from the baby's paternal grandfather, the Prince of Wales. Clearly overwhelmed, he said: 'Both my wife and I are overjoyed at the arrival of my first grandchild,' adding, 'Grandparenthood is a unique moment in anyone's life, as countless kind people have told me in recent months, so I am enormously proud and happy to be a grandfather for the first time.'

Whilst Charles and Camilla were in Canada on a four-day visit in May 2014, the Prince of Wales delivered an impassioned plea to the Canadian people to be 'mindful of the wellbeing of all our grandchildren'. He has long been an environmental advocate, and spoke of the 'huge challenges' facing the world, including youth unemployment, the growing gap between rich and poor, the need to increase opportunities for women and girls, climate change, the dangers of over-fishing and de-forestation, and the battle to advance human rights and democracy. He admitted that since becoming a grandfather these issues had come into even sharper focus.

Right:
The Duchess of Cambridge and the Duke and Duchess of Cornwall look on as Prince William has a word with Prince George as they leave the Church of St Mary Magdalene in Sandringham, Norfolk following Princess Charlotte's christening in July 2015.

Six months prior to Prince George's birth, The Queen overturned a 1917 decree that meant if the Duke and Duchess of Cambridge's first child had been a daughter, she would have been known as Lady, rather than Her Royal Highness. A Letters Patent issued by King George V had limited titles within the Royal Family, meaning that only a firstborn son would automatically become a Prince, and excluded all future sons and daughters from a similar title.

However, the new declaration stated that 'all the children of the eldest son of the Prince of Wales should have and enjoy the style, title and attribute of royal highness with the titular dignity of Prince or Princess prefixed to their Christian name or with such other titles of honour'.

Left: The Duke and Duchess of Cambridge and their children at Hamburg airport at the end of a three-day State visit to Germany in July 2017.

Below: Pageboy Prince George and flower-girl Princess Charlotte are helped by nanny Maria Borrallo as they arrive for the wedding of their aunt, Pippa Middleton, to James Matthews at St Mark's Church, Englefield, Berkshire on 20 May 2017.

A few days before the birth of William and Catherine's second child in 2015, Prince Charles revealed that he was hoping for a granddaughter. That hope was to become a reality when on 2 May Charlotte Elizabeth Diana was born. The 'absolutely delighted' Duke and Duchess of Cornwall met Princess Charlotte for the first time at Kensington Palace the day after her birth, as did Catherine's parents, Michael and Carole Middleton.

Had Charlotte been William and Catherine's firstborn, history would have been made, as a change to the Succession to the Crown Act in 2013 would have seen her become monarch ahead of any future brothers. However, even if William and Catherine have more sons, Princess Charlotte will always be next in line to the throne after Prince George, until he has children.

Charles is step-grandfather to his wife's five grandchildren. Camilla's son, Tom Parker Bowles, has two children: Lola, born in 2007, and Freddy, born in 2010. Camilla's daughter, Laura Lopes, is mother to a daughter, Eliza, born in January 2008, and twin boys, Gus and Louis, born in December 2009.

AT HOME IN LONDON, WALES AND SCOTLAND

Prince Charles' early years were spent at Clarence House with his parents, the imposing mansion built in 1825 by John Nash for the Duke of Clarence. It was to become his official London residence after the death of the Queen Mother in 2002. Charles, William and Harry moved into the classically proportioned building next to York House – their previous London home in St James's Palace – on 4 August 2003, the anniversary of the Queen Mother's birth. Today the Duke and Duchess of Cornwall welcome thousands of guests to their home in an official capacity, and for a few weeks each year members of the public can enjoy a guided tour of the gardens and main rooms on the ground floor of Clarence House.

During their marriage, Kensington Palace was Charles and Diana's London home and where they raised their sons. Following their separation, the Princess of Wales remained at Kensington and Charles took up residence in York House. Today the Duke and Duchess of Cornwall are regular visitors to Kensington Palace as it is now home to both Prince William and Prince Harry. The Duke and Duchess of Cambridge and their children live in the apartment which used to belong to Princess Margaret, whilst Prince Harry resides in Nottingham Cottage.

Below: Clarence House, the London home of the Prince of Wales.

On her accession, The Queen and Prince Philip moved to Buckingham Palace with their two small children, Prince Charles and Princess Anne. When he turned 21, as a mark of his adulthood, the Prince of Wales was permitted his own suite of rooms, which overlooked The Mall and St James's Park.

The original Buckingham House, built in the early 1600s, was enlarged to become the imposing Buckingham Palace by John Nash during the reign of King George IV. It was Prince Charles' great-great-great-grandmother Queen Victoria who chose it as the official home of the sovereign when she acceded to the throne in 1837; it has remained so ever since.

Left: The Prince of Wales' private residence at Llwynywermod, near Llandovery.

Below: The Duke and Duchess of Rothesay make their way to Crathie Church in Balmoral on their first wedding anniversary, 9 April 2006.

The Welsh home of the Duke and Duchess of Cornwall is Llwynywermod, near Llandovery in Carmarthenshire. Purchased in 2007 by the Duchy of Cornwall, Charles was captivated by the rolling landscape surrounding a cluster of farm buildings. The farmhouse, refurbished using local materials and a showcase for Welsh crafts, is the private residence of Charles and Camilla, and where they stay on their annual tour of Wales and during other visits to the Principality.

Like his mother and grandmother before him, the Balmoral Estate in Royal Deeside has always held a special allure for Prince Charles. Birkhall, an 18th-century stone house on the estate, is the private residence of the Duke and Duchess of Cornwall, and the former home of the Queen Mother who described it as a 'little big house'.

Every summer it is customary for the Royal Family to spend their summer break at Balmoral, and the Duke and Duchess look forward to each visit, enjoying fishing for salmon in the river Muick and walking on the heather-clad moors. It was at the tranquil Birkhall that they chose to honeymoon, embracing the clashing tartan wallpaper, threadbare carpets and cluttered rooms that preserve the essence of what the Queen Mother loved. One thing that has changed is the myriad grandfather clocks in the dining room, which now chime in unison; they never did in Charles' grandmother's day, much to her amusement.

AT HOME AT HIGHGROVE

Highgrove House near Tetbury in Gloucestershire is the English country home and regular weekend retreat of the Duke and Duchess of Cornwall.

The Duchy of Cornwall purchased the Highgrove Estate for the Prince of Wales in June 1980. Originally 'High Grove', the three-storey Georgian neo-classical house was built in the late 1790s on the site of an older property; the architect is thought to have been a local mason, Anthony Keck. Although more modest than many other royal residences, the Prince was immediately attracted to the quality of light that flooded the hall and the promise of what the neglected gardens, over which towered a 200-year-old cedar, could be.

For almost 40 years, Charles and a dedicated team – amongst them, at different times, Mollie Salisbury (wife of the 6th Marquess of Salisbury), Miriam Rothschild, Rosemary Verey and Sir Roy Strong – have devoted much time and energy to transforming the gardens, now renowned as some of the most inspiring and innovative in the United Kingdom, and reflecting the Prince's interests.

There are many highlights in the gardens, not least of all the enchanting Stumpery, a modern twist on the Victorian concept of planting ferns amongst tree stumps. Within the Stumpery are several unusual additions, including a thatched treehouse in a holly tree, aptly named 'Hollyrood House' and much enjoyed by the Prince of Wales' grandchildren.

Below: Highgrove House, the Gloucestershire home of the Prince of Wales.

The Cottage Garden comprises two very different planting styles: the colour scheme of the New Cottage Garden is inspired by the vibrant hues of Tibetan silks; the Old Cottage Garden is quintessentially English, with trees, shrubs, herbaceous plants and bulbs providing year-round colour.

The Sundial Garden, named for its sundial gifted by the Duke of Beaufort, was originally a rose garden designed by Lady Salisbury. It has since evolved to showcase a bold colour scheme at its best in the summer months. Beds are edged with box, willow structures support climbing plants, and the entire garden is lined with yew hedges clipped with 'windows' to reveal busts of the Prince of Wales at different stages of his life.

Golden yew, the only remnant of the original garden, lines the Thyme Walk which is planted with 20 different types of the herb. The golden yews are clipped into eccentric geometric shapes, the whole promenade leading towards the house and terrace, where a low fountain flows over a millstone.

Covering four acres at Highgrove is the constantly evolving landscape of the Wildflower Meadow, originally planted with a 32-species seed mixture in 1982. With oaks, chestnuts, poplars and beech trees at its heart, it is a sanctuary for wildlife throughout the seasons. Managed as a traditional hay meadow, it is cut in the summer and from September to December is grazed by sheep.

The Prince of Wales manages his gardens using strict sustainable principles, with ethical management and recycling of all waste materials that ensure the gardens work in harmony with nature. Similarly, Home Farm at Highgrove is a centre of excellence for organic farming. The Prince also ensures the farm takes an active role in preserving British breeds and rears several rare breeds of livestock here.

The gardens at Highgrove are open to the public on selected days between April and October each year, with profits donated to the Prince of Wales' Charitable Foundation, established in 1979, which supports a wide range of causes.

ROYAL DUTIES

In April 2016 Queen Elizabeth II celebrated her 90th birthday. Seven months previously, on 9 September 2015, she had reached a remarkable milestone in Britain's royal history when she became our longest-reigning monarch, exceeding the 63 years and 7 months record set by Queen Victoria. Despite her advancing years, The Queen has always shown remarkable stamina, but in 2014 Buckingham Palace announced that whilst Her Majesty would continue to serve as patron to the hundreds of charities and institutions with which she has been involved, she would now share the workload with her family. All four of The Queen's children have since taken on a more significant role in her demanding schedule, as have her grandsons Princes William and Harry. The Queen's decision followed the example set by the Duke of Edinburgh who relinquished some of his patronages when he turned 90 in 2011. In summer 2017, at the age of 96, and with the full support of The Queen, Prince Philip retired fully from public engagements, although it was reported that he may still attend some events with Her Majesty.

Prince Charles has been instilled with the expectations of constitutional traditions from an early age. A major part of the role of the heir to the throne is to support the sovereign. Stepping up to carry out more of The Queen's royal duties in recent years is something the Prince has welcomed with his customary diligence, demonstrating the unquenchable curiosity and pleasure he takes in meeting people – characteristics that come so naturally to him.

Below left: The Duke and Duchess of Cornwall welcomed King Felipe VI and Queen Letizia of Spain to Clarence House during their State visit in July 2017.

Below right: The Prince of Wales officiates at an investiture ceremony at Buckingham Palace.

In January 1995, Prince Charles was in Sydney to celebrate Australia Day. He was on a podium and about to speak when two shots were fired. The Prince's bodyguard pushed him aside then escorted him away whilst police and government officials overpowered his attacker. Charles remained calm throughout, impressing both the media and public. The 23-year-old assailant was a Cambodian student protesting the plight of refugees from his country being held in Australian detention centres. His weapon turned out to be a starting pistol and he was only charged with 'threatening behaviour'.

The Prince of Wales regularly carries out investitures on his mother's behalf, and represents her by welcoming dignitaries to the United Kingdom and attending State dinners during State visits.

Each year, the Duke and Duchess of Cornwall travel overseas at the specific request of the Foreign and Commonwealth Office, with the aim of developing British diplomatic interests and promoting the United Kingdom's profile abroad. Such occasions enable Prince Charles to meet Heads of State and senior officials, and enhance his understanding of a wide range of international issues. He also represents The Queen at a variety of other overseas events, including State funerals. In fact, his marriage to Camilla Parker Bowles in 2005 was delayed by 24 hours from the originally planned date because he was attending, in his royal capacity, the funeral of Pope John Paul II.

During The Queen's Diamond Jubilee celebrations in 2012, whilst she and the Duke of Edinburgh journeyed extensively around Britain, other senior members of the Royal Family represented her on overseas visits, with the Duke and Duchess of Cornwall being warmly welcomed in Scandinavia in March, Canada in May, and Papua New Guinea, Australia and New Zealand in November.

Below: The Queen looks delighted as she is greeted on stage by the Prince of Wales at the end of the Diamond Jubilee concert.

Following the Diamond Jubilee concert staged in front of Buckingham Palace on 4 June 2012, at the end of the evening the Prince of Wales began a charming tribute to his mother with the words, 'Your Majesty ... Mummy' – the same opening he had used at a similar event celebrating her Golden Jubilee, and which on both occasions brought a roar of approval and hearty applause from the audience. He went on to praise The Queen for her unstinting service, and thanked her and his father 'for always being there for us, for inspiring us with your selfless duty and service and for making us proud to be British'.

Since the start of her reign, The Queen has been committed to her role as Head of Commonwealth, and over the years the Prince of Wales has made numerous visits on her behalf to Commonwealth countries. In 2013 he made his debut presiding in her place at the biennial Commonwealth Heads of Government meeting that took place in Sri Lanka. He put his own stamp on the proceedings by highlighting two issues he cares about deeply: The Prince's Trust and the environment. He was invited to an executive session – which The Queen had never attended in all her years in charge – to discuss climate change, and Commonwealth government chiefs spoke openly for the first time about supporting Prince Charles as the next Head of Commonwealth, which is not an hereditary role.

In addition, he has his own responsibilities for the many charities and organisations with which he is involved, several of which have been established by the philanthropic Prince. When he takes the throne, he knows he will not have the time to be as closely involved as he has been to date as, along with aiding The Queen, his current role is defined as 'promoting and protecting the country's enduring traditions, virtues and excellence' – which amongst other things includes supporting Britain's rural communities and highlighting achievements or issues that without his support might otherwise receive little exposure.

Another role of the heir apparent is his involvement with the armed services, and the Prince of Wales holds the ranks of Admiral of the Fleet in the Royal Navy, Field Marshal in the Army and Marshal of the RAF.

The Prince attends the Remembrance Service at the Cenotaph each November as well as other commemorative events at home and abroad to pay tribute to the fallen. He also pays tribute to the dedication of British service personnel during visits to other countries, and is patron to a number of charitable organisations that care for the welfare of soldiers and their families.

He enjoys a special relationship with 22 regiments in the United Kingdom and Commonwealth, carrying out the ceremonial role of Colonel-in-Chief. Prince Charles' first role as Colonel-in-Chief was to the Royal

Left: The Prince of Wales lays a wreath during the annual Remembrance Sunday Service at the Cenotaph, London.

54

Left: President Mahinda Rajapaksa of Sri Lanka with the Prince of Wales at the Commonwealth Heads of Government meeting in 2013.

Regiment of Wales; he was appointed on 1 July 1969, the day he was invested as Prince of Wales. Each year he wears the uniform of Colonel of the Welsh Guards at the annual Trooping the Colour ceremony that marks the sovereign's official birthday.

The Prince of Wales regularly visits his regiments, meeting soldiers and their families and frequently spending time with injured soldiers – whom he often cheers further by sending them a personal letter and bottle of whisky.

Below: Prince Charles, Prince William and the Princess Royal on horseback at Trooping the Colour in 2016.

In May 2015, the Prince of Wales and his sister Princess Anne, the Princess Royal, were appointed as Commodores-in-Chief of the Royal Canadian Navy (RCN), the first time in history that members of the Royal Family have received such appointments in the RCN. The honours coincided with the 70th anniversary of the end of the Battle of the Atlantic during the Second World War, in which British and Canadian naval forces fought side by side.

PATRONAGES AND PASSIONS

The Prince of Wales is a man who speaks his mind. Unlike his mother's public neutrality on social and political issues, when he feels strongly about an issue he is not afraid to make his opinion heard. He knows how to find subject experts in the areas in which he wants to make a difference, and is a formidable force in bringing the right people together to achieve his aims.

He is also the most caring of men, and has a long history of kind and very private gestures towards those in need, whether friends or strangers – for example, writing letters of support to cancer patients he has met at receptions, and instructing his staff to keep him informed of their progress.

Over the years the Prince of Wales' wide range of interests have been reflected in The Prince's Charities, founded in 1979 as a group of not-for-profit organisations of which the Prince is patron or president. It is the largest multi-cause charitable enterprise in the United Kingdom; the Duke and Duchess of Cornwall carry out dozens of engagements each year to help raise over £100 million annually to support its initiatives at home and abroad, including for education, the arts, global environmental sustainability, the built environment, responsible business and enterprise, and rural affairs.

Left: The Prince of Wales meets students during a visit to the newly renamed Royal Drawing School in Shoreditch, East London. The charity, set up by Charles in 2000, was renamed in 2014, the first arts education institution to be permitted use of the title 'royal' since the Royal Ballet School in 1956.

The Prince of Wales is patron or president of more than 400 organisations, and president of 13 Prince's Charities, 12 of which he founded personally: The Royal Drawing School; The Prince's School of Traditional Arts; The Prince's Trust; The Prince's Teaching Institute; University of Cambridge Institute for Sustainability Leadership (CISL); The Prince's Foundation for Building Community; The Prince's Regeneration Trust; Dumfries House; In Kind Direct; Prime Cymru; The British Asian Trust; Business in the Community (BITC).

Perhaps the best known of the Prince of Wales' charities is The Prince's Trust, the seed of the idea for which was formed in 1971 when the Queen Mother wrote to her eldest grandson, who was at that time in the Royal Navy, of her concern about the high level of unemployment amongst boys leaving school. By 1974 Prince Charles was speaking publicly about his wish to assist teenagers and young adults seeking the challenge of creating small business enterprises. He set up a trust to make small grants for self-help schemes; it was the beginning of an initiative that evolved to become what may be his most acclaimed achievement to date: The Prince's Trust. It was launched in June 1976, with part of the initial funding coming from the Prince's severance pay on leaving the armed services. Over 40 years later, the good work continues, with disadvantaged young people aged 13 to 30 who are unemployed or struggling at school being helped to get into work, education or training, amongst them some who have gone on to become household names, such as actor and musician Idris Elba. The success of The Prince's Trust is testament to the Prince of Wales instinctively knowing what needs doing for the common good, and his steely determination in achieving a positive outcome.

Above: The Prince of Wales admires produce during a reception held at Clarence House to celebrate the 21st anniversary of Duchy Originals products.

The Duchy of Cornwall

As Prince of Wales, Prince Charles is the 24th Duke of Cornwall and the longest serving. In 2017 he celebrated 65 years as Duke. King George IV served 1762–1820 before becoming King, and King Edward VII 1841–1901 before ascending the throne. On his father's accession Prince William will inherit the Duchy of Cornwall, in line with the original charter that passes the Duchy to the eldest son of the monarch and heir to the throne.

The Duchy is a private estate established in 1337 by King Edward III for Prince Edward, his son and heir. Its operations have changed in line with aspirations of each Duke of Cornwall, but its revenue funds the public, charitable and private activities of the Prince of Wales and his family. The Duchy Estate does not cover all of Cornwall but does extend beyond its geographical boundaries, covering over 130,000 acres across several counties, mostly in south-west England.

The food brand Duchy Originals was conceived in 1990 as an outlet for organic products grown at Highgrove, with oaten biscuits being the first item sold at high-end stores such as Harrods and Fortnum & Mason. The brand has evolved over the years and today Waitrose Duchy Organic products are sold exclusively at that supermarket. Duchy products are now a subsidiary of the Prince of Wales' Charitable Foundation, which receives profits generated from the sales of the royal goods.

Right: When the Duke and Duchess of Cornwall visited Porthleven in Cornwall in 2017 they were shown artwork made from wood salvaged from the devastating storms of 2014.

Poundbury in Dorset is an urban extension of the county town of Dorchester, started in 1993 and built on 400 acres of land owned by the Duchy of Cornwall, 250 acres of which are allocated to mixed-used buildings. It has been built on the principles of architecture and urban planning as championed by the Prince of Wales and challenges some of the planning assumptions of the second half of the 20th century, demonstrating that there is an alternative way to build new communities in Britain.

Land around the compact 'urban village' is used for gardens, playing fields and pastures. Buildings are traditionally Georgian in style, many of which are home to around 3,000 residents; approximately 35 per cent of the homes are planned as affordable housing for rental or shared ownership. Several eco homes have been built in Poundbury, with more planned for the development which is due for completion in 2025. Over 2,000 people are employed at the 180 individual businesses operating in Poundbury, including Dorset Cereals and Dorchester Chocolates. Construction of a primary school started in 2016 reflects the town's growing population.

The streets at Poundbury include ornamental street lanterns, cornices above doorways, a columned village hall, small shops and utilities buried from view in the winding streets which slow traffic without need for signage. Central to the development are Pummery Square and Queen Mother Square; the latter has at its heart a statue of the Prince of Wales' grandmother, unveiled by The Queen in 2016. There is also a pub called The Poet Laureate, named in honour of Ted Hughes who was a favourite of the Queen Mother, and another called The Duchess of Cornwall Inn.

Since his time as a student at Cambridge, the Prince of Wales has been urging architects to take into account the views of ordinary people when designing homes and public buildings. At a speech at the 150th anniversary of the Royal Institute of British Architects at Hampton Court Palace in 1984, he famously spoke out about the planned extension to the 19th-century National Gallery on Trafalgar Square, saying it would be a 'monstrous carbuncle on the face of a much-loved and elegant friend'. His speech had dramatic impact and the original plans were rejected, and the Prince was much encouraged by the huge amount of public support.

Below: Poundbury in Dorset.

Above: Prince Charles takes part in a chanter lesson with local schoolchildren during a visit to Dumfries House in Scotland, one of his charities. The 18th-century house, previously owned by the Bute family for over 250 years, had fallen into disrepair before it was saved following the intervention of Prince Charles. In 2012, the 2,000-acre estate opened as a centre for education and enterprise.

The Prince of Wales has always followed his father's lead as a conservationist. Since the 1970s Charles has been forceful in raising his concerns about the environment, and at a conference at the Royal Agricultural College in Cirencester in 1983, he criticised the wanton depletion of fossil fuels and attacked modern farming methods that use herbicides and pesticides. Two years later he publicly vowed he and his family would not eat genetically modified foods.

In the period 1987/88 alone, the Prince wrote more than 1,000 letters, many to government ministers, on topics that included government policies in the Middle East, South Africa and Eastern Europe, and he had a long-running dispute with Secretary of State for the Environment, Nicholas Ridley.

During the late 1980s, Prince Charles was made aware that Romania's Communist leader, Nicolae Ceausescu, was planning to destroy thousands of traditional villages in favour of 'agro-industrial' centres. With the approval of the Foreign Office, the Prince was the first prominent European to speak to Ceausescu, resulting in the plans being halted. This was a country that the Prince came to know well; he fell in love with Transylvania – its countryside abundant with rare wildlife, its pretty streets with gabled houses and pre-Industrial Revolution way of life which he holds in great affection. He now owns two properties in Romania: a renovated 18th-century cottage in a remote village that he lets to guests and a farm with a manor house in an isolated hamlet.

Above: The Prince of Wales hugs Valentine Blacker, son of a local conservationist, on a walk around the Old Town in Bucharest, Romania during a European tour in March 2017.

The Royal Family has an allegiance to homeopathy that dates back to the mid-19th century. The Queen is known to value the principles of alternative medicine and it is a philosophy that her eldest son holds very dear. At a speech given at a dinner celebrating 150 years of the British Medical Association in 1982, the Prince of Wales condemned the medical profession's failure to recognise 'the patient as a whole' and its 'outright hostility' to alternative treatments.

On a visit to the USA in November 2005, the Duke and Duchess of Cornwall spent time in the ecological friendly San Francisco, where the Prince delivered a speech blaming droughts, heatwaves and flooding on climate change, and predicted worse to come. He implored the business community to reduce energy consumption, to counteract the throwaway society in which we live and to develop long-term strategies to replenish 'natural capital'. At the end of the impassioned speech, a member of the audience shouted out, 'Come and be our President!' It brought the house down.

Just like their father, William and Harry devote their time to a portfolio of charities, and the Prince of Wales is proud of their achievements. One main charity is The Royal Foundation of The Duke and Duchess of Cambridge and Prince Harry, originally founded by the two Princes in 2009. The Foundation is the main vehicle for these young royals' philanthropic activities, for which they have chosen three areas close to their hearts: the armed forces, young people and conservation.

THE HEIR TO THE THRONE

When it comes to a question of faith, Prince Charles is a committed Anglican who on his accession will become Supreme Governor of the Church of England. However, with a deep interest in other religions, he sees the Anglican faith as only one of the common threads linking us all 'in one great and important tapestry'. During a television interview with Jonathan Dimbleby in 1994, when asked about his ultimate coronation in which he will pledge to be Defender of the Faith, the Prince famously said that he would much rather see his role 'as Defender of Faith, not THE Faith'.

As the new millennium dawned, on 1 January 2000 BBC Radio 4's *Thought for the Day* came from the Prince of Wales, recorded in advance at Highgrove. The message was explicitly Christian and highly personal in its vision, and the Prince spoke of feeling neither blindly optimistic nor despairing about the future which he saw as an opportunity to 'rediscover a much older emotion – hope'.

The Queen's quiet dignity and grace won her a place in the hearts of the British people long ago. Without doubt, when the time comes our new King will serve with a strength of character that will continue to see our Royal Family the envy of the world. When that will be is for God alone to know. The Queen has never favoured abdication; as a young girl she experienced the life-changing effect on her immediate family when in 1936 her uncle, King Edward VIII, gave up his sovereignty to marry divorcee Wallis Simpson. Princess Elizabeth's parents had to take on roles they neither expected nor wanted – that of King

and Queen – and the 10-year-old Princess became first in line to the throne. At the core of her aversion to abdication, though, is her fundamental sense of duty and the pledge she made on her 21st birthday when in a broadcast to the Commonwealth and Empire she said: 'I declare before you all that my whole life whether it be long or short shall be devoted to your service and the service of our great imperial family to which we all belong.'

Neither does Prince William wish to take the throne early. Although, like his father, William will be destined to have a far shorter reign than his grandmother, he has said he has no desire to 'climb the ladder of kingship' before his time.

The warmth of the relationship the Prince of Wales shares with his mother was clear during the BBC documentary *Elizabeth at 90: A Family Tribute*, broadcast in February 2016. Mother and son laughed and chatted as they reminisced whilst watching vintage home movies. On The Queen's 90th birthday, as she lit a ceremonial beacon in Windsor, Prince Charles wished her 'the most special and happiest of birthdays', adding 'and long may you reign over us'.

As he moves ever closer to his destiny, one thing is certain: the right woman will be by his side. With the Duchess of Cornwall – who, it is expected, will use the title HRH The Princess Consort when her husband accedes to the throne – to support him, they will make a formidable team. Together they will ensure a continuity of the British monarchy, overcoming any challenges they may face with the love and affection that so clearly binds them.

Above: Charles and Camilla arrive for the 2016 State Opening of Parliament.

When Prince Charles does eventually become sovereign, he will be the oldest person in British history to do so, a record previously held by King William IV who was crowned aged 64 in 1830. He will also have had the longest wait to fulfil that role, exceeding the 59-year wait of King Edward VII who bided his time until the death of his mother, Queen Victoria, in 1901.

Opposite page: The Queen and three heirs to the throne – Prince Charles, Prince William and Prince George – on the balcony of Buckingham Palace following Trooping the Colour in 2016.

THE ORDER OF SUCCESSION

1. HRH Prince Charles, The Prince of Wales
2. HRH Prince William of Wales, The Duke of Cambridge
3. HRH Prince George of Cambridge
4. HRH Princess Charlotte of Cambridge
5. HRH Prince Henry of Wales
6. HRH The Duke of York
7. HRH Princess Beatrice of York
8. HRH Princess Eugenie of York
9. HRH Prince Edward, The Earl of Wessex
10. James, Viscount Severn
11. Lady Louise Windsor
12. HRH Princess Anne, The Princess Royal
13. Peter Phillips
14. Savannah Phillips
15. Isla Phillips
16. Zara Tindall (née Phillips)
17. Mia Tindall
18. David Armstrong-Jones, Earl of Snowdon
19. Charles Armstrong-Jones
20. Margarita Armstrong-Jones
21. Lady Sarah Chatto
22. Samuel Chatto
23. Arthur Chatto
24. HRH Prince Richard, Duke of Gloucester
25. Alexander Windsor, Earl of Ulster

Right: The Prince of Wales and the Duchess of Cornwall in Aberdaron during their annual summer visit to Wales in 2016.

Back cover: Prince Charles in Turkey in 2015, where he and Prince Harry joined world leaders to mark the centenary of the Gallipoli landings which claimed 140,000 lives during the First World War.